SUCCESSFUL KETO

IN **30** DAYS

COPYRIGHT AND DISCLAIMER

First Published in 2021 by Low Carb Inspirations, LLC

Copyright©Jennifer Marie Garza and Low Carb Inspirations, LLC

All rights reserved

No parts of this book may be reproduced or distributed without the written permission from the publisher.

The authors are not licensed practitioners, physicians or medical professionals. This guide does not offer medical advice, diagnoses, treatments, suggestions, or counseling of any kind. Please consult your physician before starting a new diet plan.

The information presented herein has not been evaluated by the U.S. Food and Drug Administration and is not intended to diagnose, treat, cure or prevent any disease.

The authors claim no responsibility to any person(s) or entity for any liability, loss, or damage caused or alleged to be caused directly or indirectly as a result of use, application or interpretation of the information provided within this book.

Always consult with your doctor or health care professional before starting a new diet or lifestyle change.

Table of Contents

- 05 Welcome
- 06 How to Use this Guide
- 06 Where to Get Support
- 07 The Keto Diet Plan
- 08 Supplements Required
- 09 Calculating Macros
- 10 Meal Prep Tips
- 12 Holidays and Celebrations
- 13 Weight Loss Tracker
- 14 Exercise and Keto
- 15 Food List
- 17 Foods to Avoid
- 17 Food Substitutions and Swap Ideas
- 20 Convenience Food Options
- 22 Basic Recipes
- 23 Sample Keto Meal Plans
- 27 Alcohol and Keto
- 28 Special Discounts
- 28 Stress Management
- 29 Hair Loss and Keto
- 30 Conclusion
- 31 Simple Recipes
- 43 Daily Keto Journal
- 106 My Keto Meal Plan
- 110 Notes

INTRODUCTION

WELCOME!

My name is **Jennifer Marie** and I've been doing keto for years! I am here to show you that keto is sustainable and it can be easy if you just know what to do. Congratulations! Deciding to take the 30 day keto challenge is the hardest part. Your life is about to change in a really good way!

I am the author of three keto cookbooks! **Easy Keto for Busy People, Bake it Keto and Keto Chaffle Recipes!** All of them are best sellers and loved by many in the keto community. I enjoy creating recipes that help keep us on track with our healthy lifestyle. I am here to show you that being healthy doesn't have to lack in taste or fun. I create amazing low carb and keto friendly recipes without the guilt. You can find tons of free recipes on my blog at **www.LowCarbInspirations.com.**

This is a starter guide. I will provide the knowledge and the basics to get you started.

HOW TO USE THIS GUIDE

This journal is set up with tons of information in the beginning of the guide to help you understand exactly how keto works. It includes a plan, food list, and a daily journal where you will be able to track your progress and your daily affirmations. It takes 30 days to implement a new habit and this tool will lead you to the path of success.

Fill out the journal pages every day. Be sure to start with gratitude. You will be amazed at how life changing this is when you shift your mindset to a positive one! You will track your feelings, your goals, your lessons, and your successes.

This journal will lead you to understand exactly what is happening with your own body. Each body is different so it will be important to document everything.

A dream written down with a date becomes a goal. A goal broken down into steps becomes a plan. A plan backed by action makes your dreams come true and will make you successful with keto!

WHERE TO GET SUPPORT?

We welcome you to join our **Low Carb Inspiration Facebook group**. We have thousands of people in there who are willing to help you with any question you have. It's a great way to join in on the conversation and be part of a healthy lifestyle with others doing the same journey.

Ask questions in our Facebook group:

Scan the QR code
Low Carb Inspirations Facebook Group

THE KETO DIET PLAN

The keto diet plan is an eating lifestyle that reduces carbs and sugar to allow your body to get into a state of ketosis. Your body can burn two different fuel sources. It can burn glucose or ketones. The keto diet reduces inflammation which leads to disease in the body. Not only is it healthy but the side benefit is that you will lose weight. No foods are specifically keto because ketosis is a state in which your body burns fuel but there are keto friendly foods and not so friendly foods that will easily kick you out of ketosis.

The normal Standard American Diet consists of about 300 to 350 grams of carbohydrates consumed on a daily basis. If you choose to eat a keto or low carbohydrate lifestyle you will significantly reduce the number of carbohydrates you consume on a daily basies.

The keto diet restricts daily carbohydrate counts to about 20 grams of carbs a day! If you choose a less restrictive plan this would be considered a low carb lifestyle with can range from 50 grams to 100 grams of carbs a day. Think of it this way, any amount of carbs that's lower than 300 is already a good start to a healthy lifestyle.

DIFFERENT KETO AND LOW CARB LIFESTYLE PLANS

Strict Keto	Eat healthy non processed foods and stay under 20 grams of carbs a day. The strict keto individual will always avoid foods that cause inflammation. No processed foods.
Lazy Keto	Prefers not to track all macronutrients but rather only tracks carbs and makes sure to stay under the 20 grams of carbs in a day while still eating keto friendly foods.
Dirty Keto	If you follow this plan, you don't care as much about the ingredients or the processed foods but you will still stay within the 20 grams of carbs in a day.
Low Carb Lifestyle	If you consume anywhere from 50 grams of carbs to 100 grams of carbs in a day, this is considered a low carb lifestyle. Usually, people who lose the weight they want tend to lean towards a low carb lifestyle, which is less restrictive, to help maintain their successful weight loss from the keto diet.

SUPPLEMENTS REQUIRED

The Importance of Electrolytes

The keto diet is considered a flushing diet. You will release so much inflammation in the beginning of this diet and this will cause you to have an electrolyte imbalance because you are flushing out your minerals with that inflammation.

It is super important that you take supplements while doing the keto diet. Most people do very well with taken Keto electrolytes that contain sodium, magnesium, and potassium. See the special discounts section of this book for electrolyte options.

If your electrolytes are off you can experience the Keto flu. You will feel light headed. You may have brain fog or even heart palpitations from a lack of these important minerals your body needs.

I always use Pink Himalayan salt because it has 84 minerals our body's need. I always use extra salt because the salt helps hold some of the water in so I don't get dehydrated when doing the keto diet. Specialty drinks such as Powerade Zero, which don't contain sugar, still don't have enough electrolytes that you need.

The potassium will help keep your muscles from twitching and the magnesium will help you have healthy bowel movements and less anxiety.

I have found most people to be deficient in magnesium and potassium even before starting the keto diet.

Amounts needed

Sodium (Na) is about 5000 to 7000 mg a day
Magnesium (Mg) is about 300 to 500 mgs a day
Potassium (K) is about 1000 to 3500 mgs a day.

Scan the QR code
Homemade Electrolyte Drink Recipe

Vitamin D

In my research, I have found that most Americans are deficient in Vitamin D. Vitamin D is required for your hormones to work correctly. I learned this the hard way. Be sure to consult your doctor.

I was told my naturopath doctor that vitamin d levels should be between 50 and 80 instead of the chart listed below. I started at a level of 23 and my hormones were not working correctly. I've increased my vitamin d level significantly and found huge benefits! My nails are stronger. I have more energy. My hair and skin is better.

My own doctor takes a dose of 10,000 IUs a day and his level is normal. He takes that amount just to keep up with daily needs for his body.

I have noticed a huge difference when I started taking vitamin d. My whole family takes vitamin d supplements on a daily basis. We also try and get 20 minutes of sun daily too.

Doctors use blood tests to determine if someone has adequate levels of vitamin D. They measure vitamin D using one of two measurements: nanomoles per liter (nmol/l) or nanograms per milliliter (ng/ml).

The following table provides rough ranges:

Level	Blood test result
Low	30 nmol/l or 12 ng/ml or below
Adequate	50 nmol/l or 20 ng/ml or above
High	125 nmol/l or 50 ng/ml or above

If you struggle with gut health or food digestion you might also find yourself needing to get on a prebiotic and digestive enzymes. Probiotics and digestive enzymes are not the same. Digestive enzymes are molecules which assist in the breakdown of the foods we eat, whereas probiotics are living micro-organisms which live in our gut and positively affect our body/physiological processes. Both probiotics and digestive enzymes are vital to our digestive health and perform complementary functions.

CALCULATING MACRONUTRIENTS (MACROS)

Macronutrients are protein, fat, and carbohydrates (carbs). There are two different ways to calculate your macros. You can count total carbs or net carbs.

Total carbs are all the carbs you consume in a day.

Net carbs are total carbs minus fiber and sugar alcohols = net carbs

Limiting your carbs is what puts your body into a state of ketosis where you burn fuel using ketones.

There are a few different apps you can use to track your carbs. We like to suggest **Cronometer, Carb Manager, or My Fitness Pal**. My Fitness Pal is less accurate because anyone can add macronutrients to the database.

> *It's best to recalculate your macros for every 10 lbs you lose.*

Here's how I think of macros on the keto diet.

1. **Protein is a goal.** You must always meet your protein goals so you don't lose muscle or hair.
2. **Carbs are a limit.** You don't need carbs so I treat them as a hard limit. They are there for you to consume but must be restricted to keep your body in ketosis and inflammation low.
3. **Fat is a lever.** If you have fat on your body, you will want to use this as fuel. Use fat as a lever to ward off hunger. Fat is delicious and fat can curb any appetite but use it as needed. When you first start the keto diet you might be quite hungry. Use lots of healthy fats so that you are not hungry on the plan. Once you adapt to the diet you might find that you can burn the fat stores within your body more than consuming larger amounts of healthy fats.

MEAL PREP TIPS

I find there are a few different reasons that make it difficult for people to do the keto diet. You might be really busy, have a job that keeps you on the road, work shift work, have a dairy allergy, have a nut allergy, or even the holidays or celebrations tend to throw off our healthy keto lifestyle. I will give you a few tips to help you in these situations.

Busy people guide to keto	If you lead a very busy life with kids and work, you might find it easier to prep your meals at the beginning of your week. For example, you might try batch cooking. This is where you cook all of your meats for that week on Sunday and

purchase frozen veggies that can easily be microwaved during the week. Preparing your meals ahead of time will set you up for success. It would be a great idea to have a dessert prepped ahead of time too.

Life on the road or shift work guide to keto	If you don't have an office or you are on the road all the time due to work, you might find it challenging to do keto while on the go. Most fast food restaurants will have burgers that you can order without the bun. You might even find hot dogs, hard boiled eggs, pork rinds, cheese sticks, and pork rinds at gas stations. Most restaurants will serve some sort of protein with a vegetable. The hardest part might be finding healthy fat options. Avocado is a great healthy fat option found in restaurants.
Keto on a budget	Higher quality foods can be expensive. This is a problem for many. This is why some people choose to do a dirty keto lifestyle and still have success. Please don't let your budget stop you from a life-changing shift. Eggs, hot dogs, and ground beef are easy to fit in your budget. Start off with ingredients you can afford. You will soon find that you are eating a lot less and your food bill will go down. Then you can focus on higher quality choices as your budget allows. Spend more on high quality, healthy fat options first.
Dairy free guide to keto	Dairy free keto is a bit more restrictive but definitely doable. You will find unsweetened coconut milk or unsweetened coconut cream as a really good alternatives. Your main food sources will be protein, vegetables and healthy fats. Keto can be done successfully without dairy.
Nut allergy guide to keto	I have found that coconut flour and sunflower flour are really good alternatives if you have a nut allergy. Coconut flour can be drying so it's not a one to one replacement to any nut flour. I find I use about a 1/4 of coconut flour to anything with 1 cup of almond (or another keto) flour. I really like using sunflower flour instead because it does seem to be a 1 to 1 ratio when I use it as a replacement to other keto flour options. You will have to test this for yourself.

Meal prepping tips and tools	There are lots of recipes that you can make ahead of time if you are meal prepping. You might also invest in a slow cooker or a pressure cooker or even an air fryer if you are pressed for time. We offer these types of recipes on the blog at **www.LowCarbInspirations.com**

HOLIDAYS AND CELEBRATIONS

Most people will decide ahead of time whether they want to indulge during these special occasions or stay on track. It's totally up to you. The success of staying on track may depend on your personality. If you know you can indulge for one meal and get right back to the plan, then you will have success. If you are the type of person that may struggle getting back on plan after you indulge, you may reconsider and stick to keto friendly food options. I personally did not indulge for the first 3 years of my journey. I was too afraid that I wouldn't come back from a treat meal.

Mindset hack

Be sure if you intentionally plan to have a non keto meal to call it a treat and not a cheat. A cheat indicates that you have done something wrong. If you have intentionally set out to indulge in a meal that is not keto friendly you should refer to it as a treat. Your mind will automatically think of a treat as something special and rare! It's great to keep a positive mindset during lifestyle changes.

Intermittent Fasting

Intermittent Fasting (IF for short) has a lot of wonderful benefits but it's not completely necessary as you are just starting to do a new keto lifestyle. If you choose to do intermittent fasting, it can really speed up your weight loss and help with loose skin problems you may face after a huge amount of weight loss.

There are a few different options for fasting but the one I always recommend for beginners is the 16:8 plan. This means you fast for 16 hours of the day and your eating window is 8 hours. I still use this fasting plan today and I have been doing keto for years! It's probably the easiest IF plan out there. A typical day doing the 16:8 IF plan looks like this: Wake up at 7am. Fast with only water, tea, or black coffee with no cream until 11am. First meal is either breakfast or lunch at 11am. Then stop eating your last meal at 7pm.

Intermittent fasting allows your body enough time to process the food you ate allowing your glucose to process correctly. Anyone who is at least 30 lbs or more overweight struggles with insulin resistance. Fasting allows your body to process insulin correctly by depleting the glucose from your meals. Insulin is a fat storing hormone. When you deplete your glucose from the food you eat on a daily basis, the fat storing hormone is not at work. This will stop your fat storing insulin hormone from needing to store fat and open up your cells to start burning the fat you already have for the fuel that your body needs.

The easiest way to think about the fat storing hormone insulin is that you can only burn stored body fat while in a fasted state. This is exactly why intermittent fasting is so popular. This subject is a huge one and could be a whole book in itself. If you want to learn more about Intermittent Fasting you can join the conversation in our Facebook Intermittent Fasting Rules group here for more support: **https://www.facebook.com/groups/IntermittentFastingRules/**

WEIGHT LOSS TRACKER

When you set goals to lose weight you can also set up a reward system when you reach each goal. For example, each time you lose 5 lbs think of something special you can do for yourself. This will help to keep you motivated during this health journey!

We have created a special Weight Loss Tracker that you can customize to your needs. Head over to **https://lowcarbinspirations.com/free-weight-loss-tracker/** and add your goals and rewards! This will allow you to print out your very own tracker personalized to you!

Scan the QR code
Weight Loss Tracker

EXERCISE AND KETO

If you are not used to exercising I would not recommend starting a rigorous plan when you start the keto diet. It's already challenging to change the way you eat and you don't want to add extra stress when you don't need to. Changing the way you eat will have such a positive impact on your life already! Wait until you have the plan down before adding any new goals to your lifestyle.

If you are comfortable with adding exercise to your routine, I highly suggest you start out walking. I start every morning with my daily walk. I never miss a day. Even if I am traveling, I will always walk!

You will also benefit from doing calisthenics workouts. This is where you train using your own body weight.

Another favorite of mine is body pump. It's a great way to incorporate weight lifting because it is a fast-paced, barbell-based workout that's specifically designed to help you get lean, toned and fit but I wouldn't do this if you are just starting out.

Benefits of daily walking: If you have a routine where you walk first thing in the morning it really helps to get your metabolism working, reduces cortisol, and helps deplete any leftover glycogen that may not have been used up in your system.

Weight loss hack: If you indulge in a treat meal, the quickest way to help burn off the extra sugar from overwhelming your system and triggering insulin (the fat storing hormone) is to walk off the sugar or carbs! Walk immediately after consuming the meal and it will reduce the glucose built up in your system from the meal you just ate. If you know you are going to indulge ahead of time, you might even do some light weight lifting before you go. This will open up space in your cells to be able to handle the extra glucose you are about to consume too! These are two really good ways to help keep your glucose numbers from spiking and triggering the fat storing hormone, insulin that causes you to gain weight.

I have personally used a continuous glucose monitor to really understand how the body works when you consume treat meals while doing the keto diet. These above hacks can be very beneficial for anyone who battles with insulin resistance too!

FOOD LIST

- **HWC (heavy whipping cream)** is good in coffee or whatever you would like to use it for.
- **Meat, cheese, eggs, vegetable, nuts, and healthy fats.** It's simple. Stick to that, and you should be ok!
- **Limit fruit, Berries in moderation** (strawberries, raspberries, blueberries, blackberries).

Meats

- **Beef-** Ground beef, Steak, Ribs, and Roasts
- **Pork-** Chops, Ribs, BACON, Loins, sausage
- **Chicken/Turkey-** Thighs with skin or wings are the best because breasts are high in protein. However, you CAN eat breasts, just have to eat more fat to compensate.
- **Fish-** Tuna, Salmon, Cod, Haddock, etc.
- **Shrimp/Lobster-** Go crazy, use lots of butter!
- **Pepperoni**
- **Cheese-** MOST are no carb, almost all are low carb.
- **Mozzarella & Cheddar-** Buy in bulk, they freeze well and are insanely versatile!
- **Colby jack, Pepper jack, Monterrey jack**
- **Taco style, Mexican style**
- **Parmesan, Asiago**
- **Ricotta-** Freezes well, very versatile.
- **Cottage cheese-** Good to throw in your lunch with berries, usually around 4-8g of Carbs per serving.
- **Cream Cheese-** Freezes very well, this is one of the things that I always glance at whenever I go to the store, and always buy a bunch of if it's under 75 cents per 8oz.

Vegetables

- **Leafy greens-** Spinach, Spring mix, Kale, Romaine.
- **Zucchini-** Great for a noodle substitute!
- **Avocado-** Awesome source of natural fat!
- **Eggplant**
- **Brussels sprouts**
- **Tomato**
- **Spaghetti Squash-** Versatile, makes a great spaghetti substitute and is even great for making hash browns!
- **Cucumber**
- **Peppers-** Jalapeño, banana, green/red/yellow/orange bell
- **Broccoli-** Great with cheese, steamed or just raw!
- **Asparagus-** Awesome roasted or sautéed with bacon and garlic!
- **Cauliflower-** AWESOME potato substitute!!

- **Celery**- Great with cream cheese or all natural peanut butter!
- **Cabbage**
- **Pickles** (Read nutrition labels, watch for sugar and carbs)
- **Olives**
- **Green beans**- Awesome sautéed in bacon grease with garlic, (watch portion size, though).
- **Onions**- Red, yellow: use somewhat sparingly, to taste

Fruits

Most are a no-no, especially bananas, oranges and grapes because of the high carbs and sugar.

- Strawberries
- Blueberries
- Raspberries
- Blackberries
- **Lemon/Limes**- Adds great flavor!

Nuts

Grams of Carbs per 100 grams, or 3.5 oz.

- **Pecans/ Brazil** (4g)
- **Macadamia** (5g)
- **Hazelnut/Walnut/Peanut** (7g)
- **Pine** (9g)
- **Almond** (10g)
- **Pistachio** (18g)
- **Cashew** (27g)
- Oils/Fats
- Coconut Oil
- **Butter**- Kerry Gold is best but just make sure it's REAL butter and not a spread or margarine
- Olive Oil
- Avocado oil
- Vinaigrette
- Hollandaise
- Bacon/sausage grease
- **MCT oil**- easily ordered online/in specialty stores

Dressings/Condiments/Fats

- **Ranch, Blue cheese, Cesar, Thousand Island, Balsamic**- Watch carbs/ sugar, but there's tons of brands, so you can find one you love!
- Mayo
- Aioli
- **Heinz "NO SUGAR ADDED"** Ketchup or sugar free ketchup
- **G. Hughes brand sugar free BBQ sauce**
- Yellow/Spicy Brown Mustard
- Soy sauce or coconut aminos
- Hot sauce

Liquids

Use as base for sauces/soups

- **Heavy Whipping Cream (HWC)**
- **Broths/Stocks**- Stay away from reduced fat. Bone broth is awesome!

Snacks

- Pepperoni
- **Slim Jims/jerky** (watch carbs)
- Homemade baked cheese
- Cheese

FOODS TO AVOID

- ☒ No wheat
- ☒ No sugar
- ☒ No grains
- ☒ No pasta
- ☒ No potatoes
- ☒ No rice
- ☒ No beans
- ☒ No starches
- ☒ **No milk** as it's loaded with sugar. (unsweetened almond or coconut milk is recommended.)

Vegetables that should be avoided are:

- ☒ Sweet potatoes
- ☒ Corn
- ☒ Peas
- ☒ Potatoes
- ☒ **Carrots**- can be used in moderation, just don't go over board. They are full of starches and not recommended.

TIP

Just because a product states it is keto on the package label doesn't always mean it's keto friendly. Ingredients matter! For example, one ingredient that will always cause a glucose spike is maltodextrin and it's in more products than we realize! It triggers insulin, the fat storing hormone

Stay Hydrated! Make sure to drink half your body weight In oz of water as well if you aren't getting the adequate amount of water it can be bad for your kidneys! For example if you weight 200 lbs, you will want to drink at least 100 oz of water a day.

FOOD SUBSTITUTIONS

Keto Swaps

- Wheat or white flour for almond, coconut or sunflower flour
- Real sugar for keto substitutes such as stevia, monk fruit, allulose, erythritol, etc.
- Rice, grains, potatoes for non starchy vegetables such as cauliflower, broccoli, zucchini, eggplant, onions, artichokes, cauliflower-rice, radishes (cooked radishes actually taste like potatoes believe it or not).
- Mashed cauliflower, rutabaga, or turnips are a good replacement for mashed potatoes.
- Real bread for keto bread or lower carb store-bought bread options such as keto bread (found at Costco or Aldis) or Sola bread. Most stores even carry low carb tortillas if you follow a dirty keto plan.
- You can also replace the bun on your burger with lettuce wraps of chaffle bread too (include chaffle basic recipe)

Scan the QR code
Keto Bread Options

- Tacos, wraps and tortillas: use lettuce, kale, cabbage or cauliflower wraps or even low carb tortillas if you follow a dirty Keto plan.

- Bread crumbs - use pork rinds or a mixture of Parmesan cheese and almond flour to make a crust on veggies or meats in place of pork rinds.

- Crouton's replacement can be pumpkin seeds, sliced almonds, walnuts or peanuts. Bacon bits. Crispy fried cheese crumbled or sunflower seeds.

- Pizza - use **Fat head dough recipe**. or use a **Meat pizza crust recipe**.

- Cauliflower crust recipe found in the basics of this book or use Portobello mushrooms as a base for your pizza crust.

- Real pasta for keto friendly pasta such as zucchini, carrot, turnip, rutabaga spiralized noodles. They even make Miracle noodles (shirataki noodles) that are made out of mushrooms with little taste so they take on the taste of the seasonings you add to your dish. Spaghetti squash is also a nice replacement for noodles when making spaghetti.

- Use a simple keto friendly **lasagna noodle recipe**.

- You can also use zucchini, squash or eggplant as a substitute for lasagna noodles too.

Scan the QR codes

Fat Head Dough Recipe

Meat Pizza Crust Recipe

Lasagna Noodles Recipe

- Dairy swaps if you are intolerant: Swap cheese for nuts such as pecans, pistachios, almonds and macadamia nuts. Dairy is permitted on keto if you are tolerant.

- You can also use cashew, almond or coconut milk as long as it's unsweetened.

- Crunchy chips can be replaced with baked cheese because it gets really crunchy! Add some everything bagel seasoning or jalapenos to your cheese before you bake or microwave it for extra flavor. Microwaved or baked pepperoni chips are also really crunchy and delicious!

- Celery with cream cheese spread and topped with everything bagel seasoning is a crunchy snack you will enjoy!

- Pickles are another great option for a crunchy snack. You could even roll a pickle in a slice of lunch meat with cream cheese spread too.

- Breakfast cereal: replace cereal with **Homemade Chia Pudding recipe**.

- **Pancakes or waffles** using this recipe.

- Highkey also makes an instant hot cereal.

- French fries substitute: Baked carrot sticks, crispy turnip fries, crispy daikon fries, Crispy zucchini fries, or crispy green beans.

  TIP: Use an air fryer to get them crispy and use a pork rind coating or coat it with Parmesan cheese and almond flour.

- Dessert swaps: try a **Strawberry fat bomb recipe**.
  Or a chocolate chip fat bomb recipe:

- Greek yogurt (no sugar added) mixed with berries and a couple drops of keto friendly liquid sweetener.

- Berries in heavy cream with a couple drops of keto friendly sweetener.

- **Mug cakes recipes.**

- Milk replacements: replace regular milk with unsweetened almond, cashew, coconut milk or heavy whipping cream.

- Soda replacements: swap regular soda for Zevia because it's sweetened with stevia.

- Beer or sugary cocktails can be replaced with straight spirits and sugar free sparkling water or club soda.

- Low Carb Wine. Fit Wine or Dry Farms Wine are great options for wine alternatives.

- Sugar syrups can be replaced with Jordan's Skinny syrups for coffee's, teas etc.

- Coffee creamer can be replaced with heavy whipping cream or MCT Powder.

Scan the QR codes

Homemase Chia Pudding recipe

Pancakes/Waffles Recipe

Strawberry Fat Bomb Recipe

Mug Cakes Recipes

CONVENIENCE FOOD OPTIONS

- **Real Good Foods** brand makes pizzas, breakfast sandwiches, entrees, etc.
- **Lakanto brand** makes syrups, chocolate bars, and monk fruit sweetener.
- **Choczero** makes all kinds of chocolate bars that are delicious.
- **Kettle & Fire** makes keto friendly bone broths that are high quality.
- **HighKey** makes keto friendly cookies, allulose sweetener, and hot cereals.
- **Sola** makes low carb bread, granola bars and cold cereal.
- **ThinSlim** makes low carb bread.
- **Enlightened** makes delicious keto friendly ice cream.
- **Rebel** makes delicious keto friendly ice cream.
- **Quest** makes keto friendly cookies, chips, protein bars, mct powder etc.
- **Fat Snax** makes keto friendly cookies.
- **Birch Benders** makes keto friendly pancakes and waffle mix.
- **Good Dee's** makes low carb pancake mix, pre packaged muffins & cupcakes, brownies, etc.
- **Smuckers** make sugar free jellies.
- **Primal Kitchen** makes sugar free sauces and mayo.
- **Walden Farms** makes sugar free sauces and syrups.
- **Jordan's Skinny Syrups** makes sugar free syrups and flavorings
- **SoDelicious** makes unsweetened coconut and almond milk.
- **Swerve** makes keto friendly sweetener, cakes mixes etc.
- **NOW Foods** makes keto friendly sweeteners in powder and liquid form.
- **Hershey's** makes sugar free chocolate chips and sugar free chocolate syrup.
- **Two Good** makes wonderful yogurt.
- **Gatorade Zero** makes sugar free drinks.
- **Powerade Zero** makes sugar free drinks.
- **Heinz** makes no sugar added ketchup.
- **G Hughes** makes sugar free ketchup and bbq sauces.

- **AlternaSweets** makes sugar free ketchup.
- **Baby Rays** makes sugar free bbq sauce.
- **Pili Hunters** sells Pili Nuts.
- **Eden Organics** has pumpkin seeds.
- **Miracle Noodles** sells keto friendly shirataki rice and noodles.
- **Outer Aisle** sells cauliflower pizza crust and sandwich thins,
- **Lily's** makes sugar free chocolate chips in all kinds of flavors plus peanut butter cups.
- **Bake Believe** makes sugar free chocolate chips in all kinds of flavors.
- **Nush** makes keto cakes and cookies.
- **Smartcake** makes keto friendly cupcakes.
- **Bulletproof** makes cold brew, mct oil, etc.
- **Picnik** makes keto friendly coffee creamer.
- **Torani** makes sugar free syrups.
- **DaVinci** makes sugar free syrups.
- **PerfectKeto** makes nut butters, protein bars, cookies, collagen powders, keto electrolytes etc.

- **SmartSweets** makes sugar free gummies
- **SunButter** makes sunflower butter
- **Whisps** makes fried cheese chips
- **Applegate** makes uncured pepperoni, bacon, ham with no antibiotics
- **Nature's Eats** makes almond flour
- **Arrowhead Mills** makes coconut flour
- **Bob's Red Mill** makes all kinds of keto friendly flours
- **Oh Snap!** makes pre packaged pickles.
- **EPIC** makes beef jerky.
- **FOLIOS** makes cheese wraps
- **Zevia** makes stevia sweetened drinks
- **Bird's Eye** makes all sorts of frozen vegetables prepackaged and microwaveable.
- **Eggland's Best** makes pre packaged hard boiled eggs.

Scan the QR code
Keto Products

BASIC RECIPES

Here are just a few of our basic keto recipes to get your started. We have two published cookbooks you can get on Amazon or at your local Barnes & Noble book store. Easy Keto For Busy People and Bake It Keto! We also have a cookbook for chaffles you can purchase on Amazon called Keto Chaffle Recipes.

Look out for our weekly email because we offer you a new weekly meal plan each week to help you with continued success on your keto journey! You can print them off to add to your own cookbook if needed too!

- Egg Bites
- Chia Pudding
- Naked BLT Sandwich
- Roast Beef Sandwich
- Salads
- Crack Chicken
- Grilled or Baked Chicken
- Bacon Wrapped Chicken
- Hamburgers
- Hot dogs
- Pork Chops
- Baked Fish or Salmon
- Roast Beef
- Cauliflower Pizza Crust with toppings

- Wings
- Meatball Casserole
- Basic Chaffle Recipe
- Chocolate Chip Fat Bomb
- Strawberry Fat Bomb
- Birthday Cake Chaffle
- Wonder Bread Chaffle

Scan the QR codes
Basic Recipes

KETO FOR BUSY PEOPLE OR ON THE GO

	BREAKFAST	LUNCH	DINNER
SUNDAY	Coffee or Tea with MCT Oil Sausage or bacon, egg & cheese	Mixed salad with grilled chicken or seasoned ground beef and topped with ranch or bleu cheese dressing	Naked cheeseburger with lettuce, tomatoes, onions and avocado
MONDAY	Coffee or Tea with MCT Oil Sausage or bacon, egg & cheese	Mixed salad with grilled chicken or seasoned ground beef and topped with ranch or bleu cheese dressing	Grilled chicken with a side salad and guacamole
TUESDAY	Coffee or Tea with MCT Oil Sausage or bacon, egg & cheese	Mixed salad with grilled chicken or seasoned ground beef and topped with ranch or bleu cheese dressing	Steak with grilled vegetables topped with butter
WEDNESDAY	Coffee or Tea with MCT Oil Sausage or bacon, egg & cheese	Mixed salad with grilled chicken or seasoned ground beef and topped with ranch or bleu cheese dressing	Pork chops with grilled vegetables topped with avocado or butter
THURSDAY	Coffee or Tea with MCT Oil Egg and cheese omelet with your choice of protein	Mixed salad with grilled chicken or seasoned ground beef and topped with ranch or bleu cheese dressing	Fajitas with grilled vegetables or a side salad.
FRIDAY	Coffee or Tea with MCT Oil Egg and cheese omelet with your choice of protein	Mixed salad with grilled chicken or seasoned ground beef and topped with ranch or bleu cheese dressing	Grilled fish or salmon with a side salad topped with no sugar vinaigrette dressing
SATURDAY	Coffee or Tea with MCT Oil Egg and cheese omelet with your choice of protein	Mixed salad with grilled chicken or seasoned ground beef and topped with ranch or bleu cheese dressing	Grilled lemon pepper buffalo wings or salt & vinegar chicken wings with a side of celery sticks and bleu cheese dressing

Examples of Restaurants or Fast Food Options

- **McDonalds:** Naked hamburgers, cheeseburgers, breakfast sausage, egg and cheese without the muffin.
- Most sit down restaurants that serve breakfast will have eggs or omelettes.
- Most restaurants and fast food places offer salads just be sure to get it without tortilla chips or croutons.
- **Taco Salad** can be ordered with ground beef, just don't eat the taco shell.
- **Chick Fil A** offers egg, sausage or bacon breakfast bowls.
- **Chick Fil A** offers naked chicken nuggets and salads.
- **Dunkin Donuts** offers sausage, egg and cheese without the muffin.
- **Taco Bell** offers protein power bowls, just be sure to ask them not to include the rice or beans.
- **Wing stop or Buffalo Wild Wings** is a great place to get wing options.
- Most sit down restaurants offer keto friendly protein options with grilled vegetables or a salad of choice.
- Example of salads that include about 2 to 3 cups of mixed greens with cheese, cucumbers, red onion, tomatoes, avocado, banana peppers, olives.

KETO MEAL PLAN		
BREAKFAST	**LUNCH**	**DINNER**
SUNDAY — Coffee or Tea with MCT Oil Sausage or bacon, egg & cheese	Mixed salad with grilled chicken or seasoned ground beef and topped with ranch or bleu cheese dressing	Naked cheeseburger with lettuce, tomatoes, onions and avocado
MONDAY — Coffee or Tea with MCT Oil Sausage or bacon, egg & cheese	Mixed salad with grilled chicken or seasoned ground beef and topped with ranch or bleu cheese dressing	Bacon wrapped chicken with a side salad and guacamole
TUESDAY — Coffee or Tea with MCT Oil Sausage or bacon, egg & cheese	Mixed salad with grilled chicken or seasoned ground beef and topped with ranch or bleu cheese dressing	Steak with grilled vegetables topped with butter
WEDNESDAY — Coffee or Tea with MCT Oil Sausage or bacon, egg & cheese	Mixed salad with grilled chicken or seasoned ground beef and topped with ranch or bleu cheese dressing	Pork chops with grilled vegetables topped with avocado or butter
THURSDAY — Coffee or Tea with MCT Oil Egg and cheese omelet with your choice of protein	Mixed salad with grilled chicken or seasoned ground beef and topped with ranch or bleu cheese dressing	Fajitas with grilled vegetables or a side salad.
FRIDAY — Coffee or Tea with MCT Oil Egg and cheese omelet with your choice of protein	Mixed salad with grilled chicken or seasoned ground beef and topped with ranch or bleu cheese dressing	Grilled fish or salmon with a side salad topped with no sugar vinaigrette dressing
SATURDAY — Coffee or Tea with MCT Oil Egg and cheese omelet with your choice of protein	Mixed salad with grilled chicken or seasoned ground beef and topped with ranch or bleu cheese dressing	Grilled lemon pepper buffalo wings or salt & vinegar chicken wings with a side of celery sticks and bleu cheese dressing

Recipes

- Naked Cheeseburger
- Baked Wrapped Chicken
- Steak
- Fajitas
- Fish
- Salmon
- Chicken Wings

DAIRY FREE

	BREAKFAST	LUNCH	DINNER
SUNDAY	Coffee or Tea with MCT Oil Sausage or bacon, & egg	Mixed salad with grilled chicken or seasoned ground beef and topped with olive oil and lemon juice dressing	Naked hamburger with lettuce, tomatoes, onions and avocado
MONDAY	Coffee or Tea with MCT Oil Sausage or bacon, & egg	Mixed salad with grilled chicken or seasoned ground beef and topped with olive oil and lemon juice dressing	Grilled chicken with a side salad and guacamole
TUESDAY	Coffee or Tea with MCT Oil Sausage or bacon & egg	Mixed salad with grilled chicken or seasoned ground beef and topped with olive oil and lemon juice dressing	Steak with grilled vegetables drizzled with avocado or olive oil
WEDNESDAY	Coffee or Tea with MCT Oil Sausage or bacon & egg	Mixed salad with grilled chicken or seasoned ground beef and topped with olive oil and lemon juice dressing	Pork chops with grilled vegetables drizzled with avocado or olive oil and a side of avocado slices
THURSDAY	Coffee or Tea with MCT Oil Scrambled eggs with hot sauce and your choice of protein	Mixed salad with grilled chicken or seasoned ground beef and topped with olive oil and lemon juice dressing	Fajitas with grilled vegetables or a side salad topped with no sugar vinaigrette dressing
FRIDAY	Coffee or Tea with MCT Oil Scrambled eggs with hot sauce and your choice of protein	Mixed salad with grilled chicken or seasoned ground beef add olive oil and lemon juice dressing	Grilled fish or salmon with a side salad topped with no sugar vinaigrette dressing
SATURDAY	Coffee or Tea with MCT Oil Scrambled eggs with hot sauce and your choice of protein	Mixed salad with grilled chicken or seasoned ground beef add olive oil and lemon juice dressing	Grilled lemon pepper buffalo wings or salt & vinegar chicken wings with a side of celery sticks and bleu cheese dressing

Scan the QR code

Dairy Free and Egg Free Chaffle Keto Bread Recipe

LOWCARBINSPIRATIONS.COM | PAGE 26

ALCOHOL AND KETO

Disclaimer

Consumption of alcoholic beverages impairs your ability to drive a vehicle or operate machinery, and may cause health problems if consumed in excess. While doing the keto diet you will need to significantly reduce the amount of alcohol you consume to get intoxicated. Women should not drink alcoholic beverages during pregnancy. Please drink responsibly and never drink and drive.

Alcohol is permitted on the keto diet.

Be sure the drinks you consume do not contain sugar or are high in carbs. Drinking alcohol while doing the keto diet will need some caution when you drink because it will take less alcohol to get you intoxicated.

Scan the QR code
Keto Diet and Alcohol

Better drink options

- Dry wines usually contain less than 0.5 grams of carbs per glass.
- Vodka and sugar free soda water and lemon or lime
- Whiskey
- Cognac
- Gin
- Dry martini
- Brandy
- Tequila shot
- Michelob Ultra
- Busch Light
- Miller Lite
- Medium carb count choices:
- Margarita contains about 8 carbs
- Bloody Mary contains about 7 carbs

Alcohol to be avoided

- Beer because it is made from grains unless it's a low carb beer.
- Dessert wines are high in sugar.
- Cosmopolitan
- White Russian
- Vodka and orange juice

I would personally avoid keto in the first 30 days for success. It might hinder your progress.

SPECIAL DISCOUNTS

Head over to our website and get the direct links for special discounts on keto friendly products just for being part of our group.

Scan the QR code
Keto & Low Carb Discounts

STRESS MANAGEMENT

As we all know, stress can raise the cortisol levels and put a halt on your weight loss goals. It's very important to reduce stress in your daily lives as much as possible. This subject was worthy of its own chapter. That's how important stress is to our health journey.

The first way to manage stress is to make sure you are getting adequate sleep each night. If you struggle with sleep. Try to keep a consistent sleep schedule during this challenge to improve your sleep patterns. Don't look at your phones or anything with light at least 2 hours before bedtime. Make sure your bedroom is free from all noises that could interrupt your sleep. If you have shift work hours and sleep during daylight, this could be your biggest struggle. Be sure to cover your windows with black out curtains to take out all of the light from your bedroom. Try sleeping with a box fan for white noise to drown out other noises in the house that could interrupt you. Sleep is very important and it's the first step in lowering your stress levels.

Walking can reduce stress. If you find you've had an extra stressful day, take a walk out in the sunlight for a minimum of 20 minutes. You will also benefit from the vitamin d you will get from the sun that will change your mood.

HAIR LOSS AND KETO

Anytime your body goes through a major change you might be one of those people who will experience hair loss. This is quite normal. Don't worry though, the change is temporary!

This might happen to you three to six months into your new health journey. The good news is that not only is it temporary but your hair will grow back stronger and healthier than it was before.

Here are a few reasons why you might be losing hair.

1. **When you reduce your calories and stress your body with healthy food (in a good way like this keto diet) your body will spend less energy on non-vital systems such as hair growth.** It will be super important to eat high quality foods because your consumption on the keto diet is a lot less than what you would normally eat before you started.

2. **Be careful of vitamin and mineral deficiencies.** Lack of amino acids and micronutrients such as zinc could be responsible for thinning hair. Remember when I told you that keto is a flushing diet? All of those minerals can get flushed out during the first stages of this plan. Hair health is another reason to make sure your electrolytes are balanced. Foods high in zinc are Lamb, grass-fed beef, cacao powder, pumpkin seeds, cashews, mushrooms and chicken.

3. **Stress management.** As said in the chapter previous to this one, stress management is super important. Reduce stress as much as possible to avoid hair loss too.

4. **Biotin Supplement: Biotin, Vitamin H, helps your body convert food into energy.** If you are experiencing hair loss or thinning hair, supplement with Biotin. There are certain foods that are higher in biotin such as: cauliflower, eggs, salmon, almonds, avocados, mushrooms, and spinach. Adults usually need about 30 micrograms of biotin every day.

5. **Make sure you are consuming your protein goals.** Protein is very important for healthy hair growth.

6. **Collagen Supplement: Take a collagen supplement or try consuming bone broth to help keep your hair healthy.** Bone Broth has a good amount of nutrients and will help provide the nutrients you need for beautiful hair growth. I usually consume about a 1/2 a cup a day. The older you get the less natural collagen you produce.

> *Don't let hair loss stop you from doing the keto diet! It happens to some and is very common but it is also temporary.*

CONCLUSION

Please utilize the online groups for support as needed. We want to be there for you on your road to success with the keto diet! We are on the journey with you!

Be sure to share before and after photos, lessons learned, your stories and your success! We want to be your biggest cheerleader!

Simple RECIPES

SIMPLE RECIPES

Bacon Wrapped Chicken Breasts

Serves 4 | Calories 566 | Total C 2g | Fiber 0.5g
Net C 1.5g | Sugars 0.7g | Fat 29.5g | Protein 68.5g

INGREDIENTS

- 4 chicken breasts
- 8 to 12 slices of thin bacon
- 1 teaspoon salt
- 1 teaspoon pepper
- 1/2 teaspoon garlic powder
- 1 teaspoon smoked paprika
- 1/2 tsp onion powder
- 1/4 teaspoon cayenne pepper

DIRECTIONS

1. Preheat the oven to 375 degrees F.
2. In a small bowl, combine all the seasonings.
3. Sprinkle the seasonings onto the chicken breasts evenly.
4. Wrap each chicken breast with at least two strips of thin sliced bacon.
5. Place the chicken breasts in a baking sheet with the bacon strip tucked under the breasts to keep it in place.
6. Bake for 25 to 30 minutes or until the bacon is crispy and the chicken is fully cooked through.
7. For extra crispy bacon, broil for 1 to 2 minutes after.

SIMPLE RECIPES

Hamburgers or Cheeseburgers

Serves 4 | Calories 165 | Total C 1.5g | Fiber 0.2g
Net C 1.3g | Sugars 0.1g | Fat 4.8g | Protein 25.6g

INGREDIENTS

- 1 pound ground beef
- 1/2 cup shredded cheddar cheese, if using
- 1/2 cup bacon bits
- 2 tablespoons mustard or horseradish
- 1/2 teaspoon garlic powder
- 1/2 teaspoon pink salt
- 1/2 teaspoon ground black pepper

DIRECTIONS

1. Preheat an outdoor grill to medium-high heat and lightly oil the grate or use a frying pan. Cast iron is amazing for burgers too!
2. Mix ground beef, cheddar cheese, bacon bits, mustard or horseradish, garlic powder, pink salt, and pepper in a large bowl. Divide beef mixture into 4 equal parts and shape into patties.
3. Grill or fry for about 5 to 7 minutes per side. Use an instant-read thermometer inserted into the center should read at least 160 degrees F (70 degrees C) for well-done.
4. Serve with cheese, if using.

SIMPLE RECIPES

Easy Ribeye Steak

Serves 4 | Calories 640 | Total C 0.6g | Fiber 0.2g
Net C 0.4g | Sugars 0g | Fat 33.4g | Protein 84.9g

INGREDIENTS

- 4 (8 ounce) ribeye steaks
- 1 tablespoon kosher salt
- 1 1/2 teaspoons ground black pepper
- 1 tablespoon avocado or olive oil, or as needed
- 2 tablespoons unsalted butter

DIRECTIONS

1. Two days before cooking, salt both sides of each steak with 1/2 teaspoon kosher salt per steak.
2. Place steaks in an airtight container and refrigerate until ready to cook. This is key to an amazing steak!
3. Remove the steaks from the refrigerator about 30 minutes prior to cooking. Sprinkle both sides of steak with black pepper. Allow the steaks to come to room temp so they cook evenly.
4. Heat cast iron pan over medium-high heat until very hot. Add oil and heat until oil is hot and slides down the pan easily.
5. Carefully place steaks in the cast iron skillet pan. Cook until brown and hard-seared on one side, about 4 to 5 minutes.
6. Turn steaks and top with one teaspoon butter. Cook for 3 to 4 more minutes or to desired doneness. You may need to cook the steaks in batches depending on the size of your cast iron pan.

SIMPLE RECIPES

Easy Tilapia

Serves 4 | Calories 202 | Total C 0.6g | Fiber 0.1g
Net C 0.5g | Sugars 0.2g | Fat 9.5g | Protein 27g

INGREDIENTS

- 1 pound tilapia fillets
- 3 tablespoons parmesan cheese
- 1 tablespoon butter, softened
- 1 tablespoon mayonnaise
- 1 tablespoon fresh lemon juice
- 1/4 teaspoon dried basil
- 1/4 teaspoon ground black pepper
- 1/8 teaspoon onion powder

DIRECTIONS

1. Preheat oven broiler. Grease a broiling pan or line with aluminum foil.

2. Mix parmesan cheese, butter, mayonnaise, and lemon juice together in a small bowl. Season with dried basil, pepper, and onion powder. Mix well and set aside. Arrange fillets in a single layer on the prepared pan.

3. Broil a few inches from the heat for 2 to 3 minutes. Flip fillets over and broil for 2 or 3 minutes more. Remove fillets from the oven and cover with parmesan mixture on top side. Broil until fish flakes easily with a fork, about 2 minutes.

SIMPLE RECIPES

Baked Salmon

Serves 4 | Calories 704 | Total C 1.2g | Fiber 0.2g
Net C 1g | Sugars 0.1g | Fat 39.6g | Protein 88.3g

INGREDIENTS

- 2 (6 ounce) fillets salmon
- 2 cloves garlic, minced
- 6 tablespoons light olive oil
- 1 teaspoon dried basil
- 1 teaspoon pink salt
- 1 teaspoon ground black pepper
- 1 tablespoon lemon juice
- 1 tablespoon fresh parsley, chopped

DIRECTIONS

1. In a medium bowl or plastic bag, mix the garlic, light olive oil, basil, salt, pepper, lemon juice and parsley to create a marinade. Place salmon fillets in the marinade. Marinate in the refrigerator for about 1 hour.
2. Preheat the oven to 425 degrees F.
3. Place fillets in a roasting pan skin side down.
4. Roast for 4 to 6 minutes per half-inch thickness of salmon: Roasting time depends on the thickness of your salmon, as determined by the thickest part of the salmon fillet.

SIMPLE RECIPES

Garlic Parmesan Chicken Wings

Serves 4 | Calories 168 | Total C 4.9g | Fiber 0.4g
Net C 4.5g | Sugars 0.2g | Fat 14.6g | Protein 6.2g

INGREDIENTS

- 2 pounds chicken wings
- 1 1/2 tablespoons baking powder
- 1 teaspoon salt
- 1/2 teaspoon pepper
- 1/4 cup butter
- 2 tablespoons minced garlic
- 2 teaspoons dried parsley
- 1 teaspoon onion powder
- 2 teaspoons red's hot sauce
- 1/2 cup grated parmesan

DIRECTIONS

1. Preheat oven to 400 degrees.
2. Line a baking sheet with foil. Spray the foil with non stick cooking spray.
3. Pat wings dry using paper towels. Add baking powder, salt, and pepper to a large zip bag. Shake to coat the chicken wings.
4. Lay wings on the prepared baking sheet and back them for about 45 minutes or until they are golden brown.
5. Transfer the cooked wings to a large bowl.
6. Melt the butter in a microwaveable safe bowl or in a saucepan. Add the garlic, parsley, onion powder and Red's hot sauce. Pour the butter sauce over the chicken wings and sprinkle with the parmesan. Toss well to coat.
7. Serve immediately with a side salad or celery sticks.

SIMPLE RECIPES

Sheet Pan Chicken Fajitas

Serves 4 | Calories 176 | Total C 5.6g | Fiber 1.8g
Net C 3.8g | Sugars 2.2g | Fat 7.9g | Protein 20.1g

INGREDIENTS

- 3/4 pounds chicken tenders, cut into thin strips
- 1 teaspoon onion powder
- 1 teaspoon chili powder
- 1 teaspoon cumin
- 1/2 teaspoon oregano
- 1/2 teaspoon smoked paprika
- 1/2 teaspoon salt
- 1/2 teaspoon pepper
- 1/2 red bell pepper
- 1/2 green bell pepper
- 1/2 yellow or orange bell pepper
- 1/2 small onion, sliced
- 1 tablespoon minced garlic
- 1 1/2 tablespoons avocado oil

DIRECTIONS

1. Preheat the oven to 425 degrees.
2. Prepare a large baking sheet by spraying it with non stick cooking oil.
3. Cut the bell peppers and onion.
4. In a small bowl combine the onion powder, chili powder, cumin, oregano, smoked paprika, salt, and pepper. Mix until combined.
5. In a large bowl add the chicken, bell peppers and onion.
6. Drizzle with avocado oil and add the minced garlic.
7. Add the dry seasonings to the mixture and toss the chicken and veggies until it's all fully coated.
8. Spread out of the prepared baking sheet and bake for 25 minutes or until chicken is fully cooked.
9. Serve over a salad and enjoy!

SIMPLE RECIPES

Easy Salad Recipe

Serves 4 | Calories 74 | Total C 3.9g | Fiber 1.1g
Net C 2.7g | Sugars 1.7g | Fat 4g | Protein 6.2g

INGREDIENTS

- 3 cups chopped lettuce or mixed greens
- 2 ounces cheese (feta, goat, mixed, parmesan, cheddar, blue cheese, etc...)
- cucumber slices
- red or green bell pepper slices
- avocado slices
- banana peppers

Optional salad toppings:
- salt
- pepper
- Everything Bagel Seasoning
- olive oil
- Infused Flavored Olive Oils (rosemary, lemon, garlic)
- Avocado Oil
- Lemon Juice
- MCT Oil
- Ranch Dressing
- Blue Cheese Dressing
- Avocado Ranch Dressing
- Greek Dressing

DIRECTIONS

1. Wash ingredients and pat dry.
2. Slice vegetables and set aside.
3. In a large salad bowl, add lettuce or mixed greens with the cheese, cucumber, red or green bell peppers, and banana peppers.
4. Toss together well.
5. Top with avocado slices.
6. Serve and top with your choice of optional salad toppings, if any.

SIMPLE RECIPES

Fatty Coffee or Tea

Serves 1 | Calories 122 | Total C 0g | Fiber 0g
Net C 0g | Sugars 0g | Fat 14g | Protein 0.3g

INGREDIENTS

- 8 ounce cup of hot black coffee or hot black tea
- 1 tablespoon MCT oil
- Optional: 1 teaspoon Jordan's Skinny syrup (any flavor you choose) or a teaspoon of your favorite keto friendly sweetener of choice.

DIRECTIONS

1. In a blender, add the hot black coffee or hot black tea with MCT Oil and optional sweetener.

2. Blend together well to allow the coffee or tea to emulsify with the MCT oil. This will make the coffee or tea a frothy texture when blended well.

    Note: Using a blender is key with this recipe. If you don't use a blender, the coffee or tea will not mix together with the oil and it will separate.

Daily KETO JOURNAL

Date: _____

TODAY I am grateful for

_____
_____
_____

My goal to **keto success** today is...

_____
_____
_____

One thing I appreciate about my **keto journey** today is

_____
_____
_____

Am I **hydrated**?

1	2	3	4	5	6	7
Good	Good	Fair	Dehydrated	Dehydrated	Very Dehydrated	Severe Dehydration

RATE YOUR DAY

MOVE Today's workout	**NOURISH** Today's food	**REFLECT** Today's mood
Number of minutes ____	Energy Level 0 5 10	😊 😐 ☹

GLUCOSE/KETONE Reading	**FASTING** Schedule	**SLEEP**

LOWCARBINSPIRATIONS.COM | PAGE 44

If you want to change your life,

YOU have the **POWER**

THIS INSPIRES ME

Date: _____

TODAY I am grateful for

_____
_____
_____

My goal to keto success today is...

_____
_____
_____

One thing I appreciate about my keto journey today is

_____
_____
_____

Am I hydrated?

1	2	3	4	5	6	7
Good	Good	Fair	Dehydrated	Dehydrated	Very Dehydrated	Severe Dehydration

RATE YOUR DAY

MOVE
Today's workout

Number of minutes _____

NOURISH
Today's food

Energy Level 0 — 5 — 10

REFLECT
Today's mood

:) :| :(

GLUCOSE/KETONE
Reading

FASTING
Schedule

SLEEP

LOWCARBINSPIRATIONS.COM | PAGE 46

LIFE begins at the end of your *comfort* **zone.**

THIS INSPIRES ME

Date: _____

TODAY I am grateful for

_____
_____

My goal to keto success today is...

_____
_____

One thing I appreciate about my keto journey today is

_____
_____

Am I hydrated?

1	2	3	4	5	6	7
Good	Good	Fair	Dehydrated	Dehydrated	Very Dehydrated	Severe Dehydration

RATE YOUR DAY

MOVE
Today's workout

Number of minutes _____

NOURISH
Today's food

Energy Level: 0 — 5 — 10

REFLECT
Today's mood

🙂 😐 🙁

GLUCOSE/KETONE
Reading

FASTING
Schedule

SLEEP

LOWCARBINSPIRATIONS.COM | PAGE 48

Strength doesn't come from what *you can do* it comes from **OVERCOMING** *the things* you ONCE thought **YOU COULDN'T**
~Rikki Rogers~

THIS INSPIRES ME

Date: _____

TODAY I am grateful for

_____
_____
_____

My goal to keto success today is...

_____
_____
_____

One thing I appreciate about my keto journey today is

_____
_____
_____

Am I hydrated?

1	2	3	4	5	6	7
Good	Good	Fair	Dehydrated	Dehydrated	Very Dehydrated	Severe Dehydration

RATE YOUR DAY

MOVE
Today's workout

Number of minutes

NOURISH
Today's food

Energy Level 0 5 10

REFLECT
Today's mood

GLUCOSE/KETONE
Reading

FASTING
Schedule

SLEEP

LOWCARBINSPIRATIONS.COM | PAGE 50

An idea is just a **dream** *until you write it down...then it's a* **GOAL**

THIS INSPIRES ME

Date: _____

TODAY I am grateful for

_____
_____
_____

My goal to **keto success** today is…

_____
_____
_____

One thing I appreciate about my **keto journey** today is

_____
_____
_____

Am I **hydrated**?

1	2	3	4	5	6	7
Good	Good	Fair	Dehydrated	Dehydrated	Very Dehydrated	Severe Dehydration

RATE YOUR DAY

MOVE
Today's workout

Number of minutes: _____

NOURISH
Today's food

Energy Level: 0 — 5 — 10

REFLECT
Today's mood

😊 😐 ☹️

GLUCOSE/KETONE
Reading

FASTING
Schedule

SLEEP

LOWCARBINSPIRATIONS.COM | PAGE 52

Love yourself and life becomes the party.

THIS INSPIRES ME

Date: _____

TODAY I am grateful for

_____
_____

My goal to keto success today is...

_____
_____

One thing I appreciate about my keto journey today is

_____
_____

Am I hydrated?

1	2	3	4	5	6	7
Good	Good	Fair	Dehydrated	Dehydrated	Very Dehydrated	Severe Dehydration

RATE YOUR DAY

MOVE
Today's workout

Number of minutes

NOURISH
Today's food

Energy Level 0 5 10

REFLECT
Today's mood

GLUCOSE/KETONE
Reading

FASTING
Schedule

SLEEP

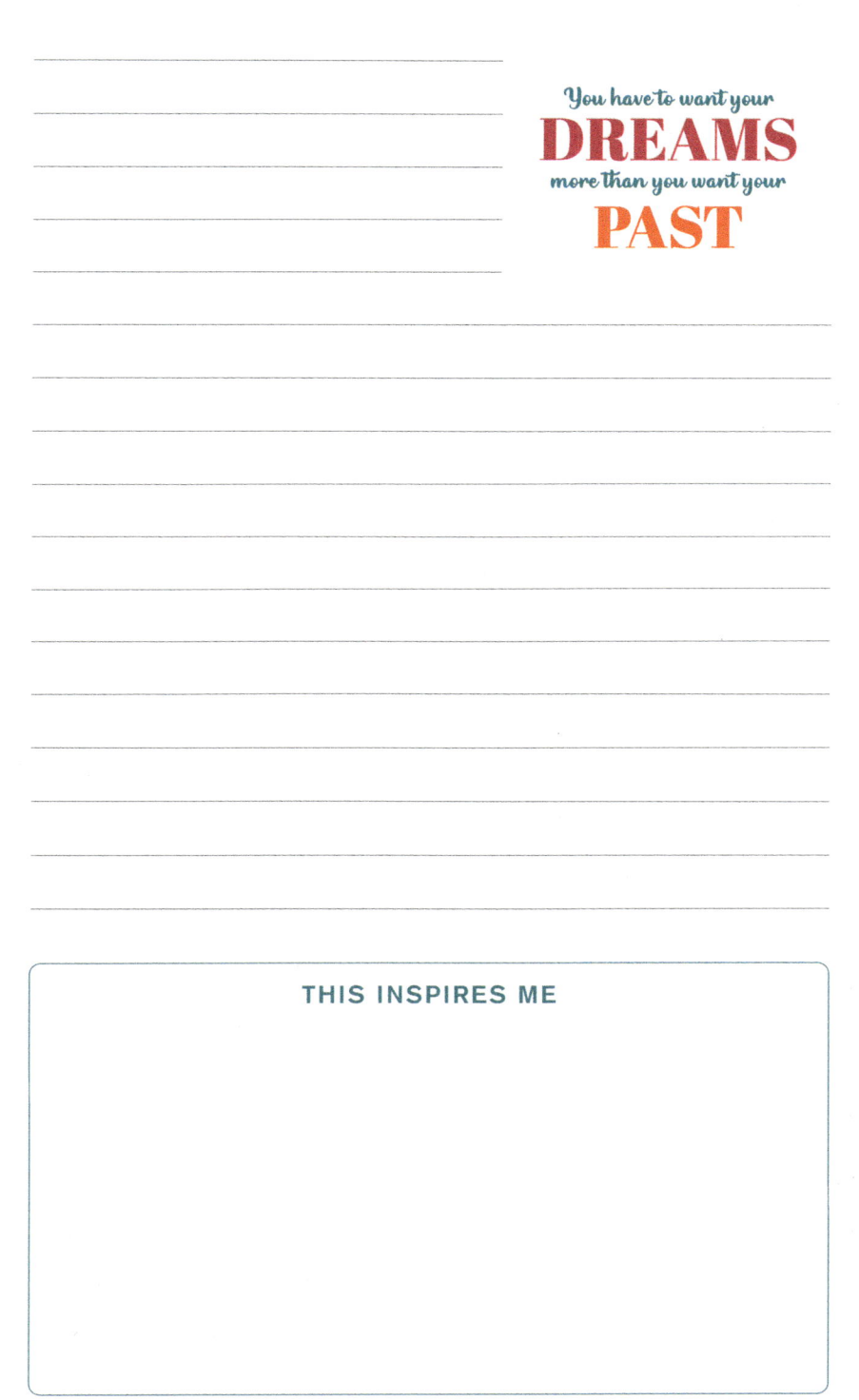

You have to want your
DREAMS
more than you want your
PAST

THIS INSPIRES ME

Date: _____

TODAY I am grateful for

_____
_____
_____

My goal to keto success today is...

_____
_____
_____

One thing I appreciate about my keto journey today is

_____
_____
_____

Am I hydrated?

1	2	3	4	5	6	7
Good	Good	Fair	Dehydrated	Dehydrated	Very Dehydrated	Severe Dehydration

RATE YOUR DAY

MOVE
Today's workout

Number of minutes _____

NOURISH
Today's food

Energy Level 0 — 5 — 10

REFLECT
Today's mood

🙂 😐 🙁

GLUCOSE/KETONE
Reading

FASTING
Schedule

SLEEP

Stay the COURSE BECAUSE YOU ARE WORTH IT.

THIS INSPIRES ME

Date: _____

TODAY I am grateful for

_____
_____
_____

My goal to keto success today is...

_____
_____
_____

One thing I appreciate about my keto journey today is

_____
_____
_____

Am I hydrated?

1	2	3	4	5	6	7
Good	Good	Fair	Dehydrated	Dehydrated	Very Dehydrated	Severe Dehydration

RATE YOUR DAY

MOVE
Today's workout

Number of minutes: ____

NOURISH
Today's food

Energy Level: 0 — 5 — 10

REFLECT
Today's mood

🙂 😐 ☹️

GLUCOSE/KETONE
Reading

FASTING
Schedule

SLEEP

> Love yourself no matter what anyone else says or thinks.

THIS INSPIRES ME

Date: _____

TODAY I am grateful for

_____
_____
_____

My goal to keto success today is...

_____
_____
_____

One thing I appreciate about my keto journey today is

_____
_____
_____

Am I hydrated?

1	2	3	4	5	6	7
Good	Good	Fair	Dehydrated	Dehydrated	Very Dehydrated	Severe Dehydration

RATE YOUR DAY

MOVE
Today's workout

Number of minutes

NOURISH
Today's food

Energy Level: 0 — 5 — 10

REFLECT
Today's mood

😊 😐 ☹️

GLUCOSE/KETONE
Reading

FASTING
Schedule

SLEEP

LOWCARBINSPIRATIONS.COM | PAGE 60

> To accomplish **great things,** you must not only **act** but also **dream** and **BELIEVE.**

THIS INSPIRES ME

Date: _____

TODAY I am grateful for

_____
_____
_____

My goal to keto success today is...

_____
_____
_____

One thing I appreciate about my **keto journey** today is

_____
_____
_____

Am I hydrated?

1	2	3	4	5	6	7
Good	Good	Fair	Dehydrated	Dehydrated	Very Dehydrated	Severe Dehydration

RATE YOUR DAY

MOVE Today's workout	**NOURISH** Today's food	**REFLECT** Today's mood
Number of minutes _____	Energy Level 0 — 5 — 10	🙂 😐 ☹️

GLUCOSE/KETONE Reading	**FASTING** Schedule	**SLEEP**

LOWCARBINSPIRATIONS.COM | PAGE 62

SLOW PROGRESS IS BETTER THAN **NO PROGRESS**

THIS INSPIRES ME

Date: _____

TODAY I am grateful for

_____
_____
_____

My goal to **keto success** today is...

_____
_____
_____

One thing I appreciate about my **keto journey** today is

_____
_____
_____

Am I **hydrated**?

1	2	3	4	5	6	7
Good	Good	Fair	Dehydrated	Dehydrated	Very Dehydrated	Severe Dehydration

RATE YOUR DAY

MOVE
Today's workout

Number of minutes

NOURISH
Today's food

Energy Level 0 5 10

REFLECT
Today's mood

GLUCOSE/KETONE
Reading

FASTING
Schedule

SLEEP

> **whether you think you can, or think you can't, you're right.**
> — Henry Ford

THIS INSPIRES ME

Date: _____

TODAY I am grateful for

_____
_____
_____

My goal to keto success today is...

_____
_____
_____

One thing I appreciate about my keto journey today is

_____
_____
_____

Am I hydrated?

1	2	3	4	5	6	7
Good	Good	Fair	Dehydrated	Dehydrated	Very Dehydrated	Severe Dehydration

RATE YOUR DAY

MOVE
Today's workout

Number of minutes _____

NOURISH
Today's food

Energy Level 0 — 5 — 10

REFLECT
Today's mood

😊 😐 ☹️

GLUCOSE/KETONE
Reading

FASTING
Schedule

SLEEP

one **bad meal** won't make you **fat** just like one **good meal** won't make you **thin**.

THIS INSPIRES ME

Date: _____

TODAY I am grateful for

_____
_____
_____

My goal to keto success today is...

_____
_____
_____

One thing I appreciate about my keto journey today is

_____
_____
_____

Am I hydrated?

1	2	3	4	5	6	7
Good	Good	Fair	Dehydrated	Dehydrated	Very Dehydrated	Severe Dehydration

RATE YOUR DAY

MOVE Today's workout	**NOURISH** Today's food	**REFLECT** Today's mood
Number of minutes ____	Energy Level 0 — 5 — 10	🙂 😐 🙁

GLUCOSE/KETONE Reading	**FASTING** Schedule	**SLEEP**

LOWCARBINSPIRATIONS.COM | PAGE 68

Let your **FAITH** *be bigger than your* **FEAR.**

THIS INSPIRES ME

Date: _____

TODAY I am grateful for

_____
_____
_____

My goal to keto success today is...

_____
_____
_____

One thing I appreciate about my keto journey today is

_____
_____
_____

Am I hydrated?

1	2	3	4	5	6	7
Good	Good	Fair	Dehydrated	Dehydrated	Very Dehydrated	Severe Dehydration

RATE YOUR DAY

MOVE
Today's workout

Number of minutes: _____

NOURISH
Today's food

Energy Level: 0 — 5 — 10

REFLECT
Today's mood

🙂 😐 🙁

GLUCOSE/KETONE
Reading

FASTING
Schedule

SLEEP

LOWCARBINSPIRATIONS.COM | PAGE 70

Success OCCURS WHEN YOUR **DREAMS** ARE BIGGER THAN YOUR *excuses.*

THIS INSPIRES ME

Date: _____

TODAY I am grateful for

_____
_____

My goal to keto success today is…

_____
_____

One thing I appreciate about my keto journey today is

_____
_____

Am I hydrated?

1	2	3	4	5	6	7
Good	Good	Fair	Dehydrated	Dehydrated	Very Dehydrated	Severe Dehydration

RATE YOUR DAY

MOVE
Today's workout

Number of minutes

NOURISH
Today's food

Energy Level 0 5 10

REFLECT
Today's mood

GLUCOSE/KETONE
Reading

FASTING
Schedule

SLEEP

LOWCARBINSPIRATIONS.COM | PAGE 72

> If you haven't felt like **QUITTING**, your dreams and goals aren't **BIG** enough.

THIS INSPIRES ME

Date: _____

TODAY I am grateful for

_____
_____
_____

My goal to keto success today is...

_____
_____
_____

One thing I appreciate about my keto journey today is

_____
_____
_____

Am I hydrated?

1	2	3	4	5	6	7
Good	Good	Fair	Dehydrated	Dehydrated	Very Dehydrated	Severe Dehydration

RATE YOUR DAY

MOVE
Today's workout

Number of minutes: _____

NOURISH
Today's food

Energy Level: 0 — 5 — 10

REFLECT
Today's mood

🙂 😐 🙁

GLUCOSE/KETONE
Reading

FASTING
Schedule

SLEEP

LOWCARBINSPIRATIONS.COM | PAGE 74

SUCCESS IS MERELY WHERE *preparation* MEETS **OPPORTUNITY.**

THIS INSPIRES ME

Date: _____

TODAY I am grateful for

_____

_____

_____

My goal to keto success today is...

_____

_____

_____

One thing I appreciate about my keto journey today is

_____

_____

_____

Am I hydrated?

1	2	3	4	5	6	7
Good	Good	Fair	Dehydrated	Dehydrated	Very Dehydrated	Severe Dehydration

RATE YOUR DAY

MOVE
Today's workout

Number of minutes: ____

NOURISH
Today's food

Energy Level: 0 — 5 — 10

REFLECT
Today's mood

🙂 😐 🙁

GLUCOSE/KETONE
Reading

FASTING
Schedule

SLEEP

LOWCARBINSPIRATIONS.COM | PAGE 76

> I'm not telling you it's going to be easy, I'm telling you it's going to be worth it.

THIS INSPIRES ME

Date: _____

TODAY I am grateful for

_____
_____
_____

My goal to keto success today is...

_____
_____
_____

One thing I appreciate about my keto journey today is

_____
_____
_____

Am I hydrated?

1	2	3	4	5	6	7
Good	Good	Fair	Dehydrated	Dehydrated	Very Dehydrated	Severe Dehydration

RATE YOUR DAY

MOVE
Today's workout

Number of minutes

NOURISH
Today's food

Energy Level: 0 — 5 — 10

REFLECT
Today's mood

😊 😐 ☹️

GLUCOSE/KETONE
Reading

FASTING
Schedule

SLEEP

LOWCARBINSPIRATIONS.COM | PAGE 78

You are going to want to give up but...

DON'T

THIS INSPIRES ME

Date: _____

TODAY I am grateful for

_____
_____
_____

My goal to keto success today is...

_____
_____
_____

One thing I appreciate about my keto journey today is

_____
_____
_____

Am I hydrated?

1	2	3	4	5	6	7
Good	Good	Fair	Dehydrated	Dehydrated	Very Dehydrated	Severe Dehydration

RATE YOUR DAY

MOVE
Today's workout

Number of minutes _____

NOURISH
Today's food

Energy Level 0 — 5 — 10

REFLECT
Today's mood

😊 😐 ☹️

GLUCOSE/KETONE
Reading

FASTING
Schedule

SLEEP

FALLING DOWN IS PART OF LIFE.

GETTING BACK UP IS LIVING

THIS INSPIRES ME

Date: _____

TODAY I am grateful for

_____
_____

My goal to keto success today is...

_____
_____

One thing I appreciate about my keto journey today is

_____
_____

Am I hydrated?

1	2	3	4	5	6	7
Good	Good	Fair	Dehydrated	Dehydrated	Very Dehydrated	Severe Dehydration

RATE YOUR DAY

MOVE
Today's workout

Number of minutes

NOURISH
Today's food

Energy Level   0   5   10

REFLECT
Today's mood

GLUCOSE/KETONE
Reading

FASTING
Schedule

SLEEP

LOWCARBINSPIRATIONS.COM | PAGE 82

strive for progress
NOT PERFECTION

THIS INSPIRES ME

Date: _____

TODAY I am grateful for

_____
_____

My goal to keto success today is...

_____
_____

One thing I appreciate about my keto journey today is

_____
_____

Am I hydrated?							
1 Good	2 Good	3 Fair	4 Dehydrated	5 Dehydrated	6 Very Dehydrated	7 Severe Dehydration	

RATE YOUR DAY

MOVE
Today's workout

Number of minutes

NOURISH
Today's food

Energy Level 0 5 10

REFLECT
Today's mood

GLUCOSE/KETONE
Reading

FASTING
Schedule

SLEEP

LOWCARBINSPIRATIONS.COM | PAGE 84

30 days of new tasks becomes a **HABIT!**

THIS INSPIRES ME

Date: _____

TODAY I am grateful for

_____
_____

My goal to **keto success** today is...

_____
_____

One thing I appreciate about my **keto journey** today is

_____
_____

Am I **hydrated**?

1	2	3	4	5	6	7
Good	Good	Fair	Dehydrated	Dehydrated	Very Dehydrated	Severe Dehydration

RATE YOUR DAY

MOVE	**NOURISH**	**REFLECT**
Today's workout	Today's food	Today's mood
Number of minutes	Energy Level 0 — 5 — 10	🙂 😐 🙁

GLUCOSE/KETONE	**FASTING**	**SLEEP**
Reading	Schedule	

LOWCARBINSPIRATIONS.COM | PAGE 86

COMMITMENT MEANS STAYING LOYAL TO WHAT YOU SAID YOU WERE GOING TO DO LONG AFTER THE MOOD YOU SAID IT IN HAS LEFT YOU.

THIS INSPIRES ME

Date: _____

TODAY I am grateful for

_____
_____
_____

My goal to keto success today is...

_____
_____
_____

One thing I appreciate about my keto journey today is

_____
_____
_____

Am I hydrated?

1	2	3	4	5	6	7
Good	Good	Fair	Dehydrated	Dehydrated	Very Dehydrated	Severe Dehydration

RATE YOUR DAY

MOVE
Today's workout

Number of minutes: _____

NOURISH
Today's food

Energy Level: 0 — 5 — 10

REFLECT
Today's mood

:) :| :(

GLUCOSE/KETONE
Reading

FASTING
Schedule

SLEEP

LOWCARBINSPIRATIONS.COM | PAGE 88

> **MOTIVATION** IS WHAT GETS YOU STARTED. **HABIT** IS WHAT KEEPS YOU GOING.
> ~JIM ROHN~

THIS INSPIRES ME

Date: _____

TODAY I am grateful for

_____
_____
_____

My goal to keto success today is...

_____
_____
_____

One thing I appreciate about my keto journey today is

_____
_____
_____

Am I hydrated?

1	2	3	4	5	6	7
Good	Good	Fair	Dehydrated	Dehydrated	Very Dehydrated	Severe Dehydration

RATE YOUR DAY

MOVE
Today's workout

Number of minutes _____

NOURISH
Today's food

Energy Level   0 — 5 — 10

REFLECT
Today's mood

🙂 😐 🙁

GLUCOSE/KETONE
Reading

FASTING
Schedule

SLEEP

LOWCARBINSPIRATIONS.COM | PAGE 90

> You have two choices:
> **MAKE PROGRESS** or **MAKE EXCUSES**
> What will you choose?

THIS INSPIRES ME

Date: _____

TODAY I am grateful for

_____
_____
_____

My goal to **keto success** today is...

_____
_____
_____

One thing I appreciate about my **keto journey** today is

_____
_____
_____

Am I hydrated?

1	2	3	4	5	6	7
Good	Good	Fair	Dehydrated	Dehydrated	Very Dehydrated	Severe Dehydration

RATE YOUR DAY

MOVE
Today's workout

Number of minutes ____

NOURISH
Today's food

Energy Level: 0 — 5 — 10

REFLECT
Today's mood

😊 😐 ☹️

GLUCOSE/KETONE
Reading

FASTING
Schedule

SLEEP

LOWCARBINSPIRATIONS.COM | PAGE 92

SET SOME GOALS THEN DEMOLISH THEM

THIS INSPIRES ME

Date: _____

TODAY I am grateful for

_____
_____
_____

My goal to **keto success** today is...

_____
_____
_____

One thing I appreciate about my **keto journey** today is

_____
_____
_____

Am I hydrated?

1	2	3	4	5	6	7
Good	Good	Fair	Dehydrated	Dehydrated	Very Dehydrated	Severe Dehydration

RATE YOUR DAY

MOVE	**NOURISH**	**REFLECT**
Today's workout	Today's food	Today's mood
Number of minutes	Energy Level 0 5 10	😊 😐 ☹️

GLUCOSE/KETONE	**FASTING**	**SLEEP**
Reading	Schedule	

LOWCARBINSPIRATIONS.COM | PAGE 94

ANYTHING worth having is WORTH working HARD for.

THIS INSPIRES ME

Date: _____

TODAY I am grateful for

_____
_____
_____

My goal to keto success today is...

_____
_____
_____

One thing I appreciate about my keto journey today is

_____
_____
_____

Am I hydrated?

1	2	3	4	5	6	7
Good	Good	Fair	Dehydrated	Dehydrated	Very Dehydrated	Severe Dehydration

RATE YOUR DAY

MOVE
Today's workout

Number of minutes _____

NOURISH
Today's food

Energy Level: 0 — 5 — 10

REFLECT
Today's mood

:) :| :(

GLUCOSE/KETONE
Reading

FASTING
Schedule

SLEEP

LOWCARBINSPIRATIONS.COM | PAGE 96

> Take pride
> IN HOW FAR
> YOU'VE COME
> AND
> HAVE FAITH
> IN HOW FAR
> YOU CAN GO

THIS INSPIRES ME

Date: _____

TODAY I am grateful for

_____
_____

My goal to keto success today is...

_____
_____

One thing I appreciate about my keto journey today is

_____
_____

Am I hydrated?							
1 Good	2 Good	3 Fair	4 Dehydrated	5 Dehydrated	6 Very Dehydrated	7 Severe Dehydration	

RATE YOUR DAY

MOVE
Today's workout

Number of minutes

NOURISH
Today's food

Energy Level 0 5 10

REFLECT
Today's mood

GLUCOSE/KETONE
Reading

FASTING
Schedule

SLEEP

LOWCARBINSPIRATIONS.COM | PAGE 98

**Turn intentions
into ACTIONS**

THIS INSPIRES ME

Date: _____

TODAY I am grateful for

_____
_____
_____

My goal to **keto success** today is...

_____
_____
_____

One thing I appreciate about my **keto journey** today is

_____
_____
_____

Am I **hydrated**?

1	2	3	4	5	6	7
Good	Good	Fair	Dehydrated	Dehydrated	Very Dehydrated	Severe Dehydration

RATE YOUR DAY

MOVE
Today's workout

Number of minutes: _____

NOURISH
Today's food

Energy Level: 0 — 5 — 10

REFLECT
Today's mood

🙂 😐 🙁

GLUCOSE/KETONE
Reading

FASTING
Schedule

SLEEP

LOWCARBINSPIRATIONS.COM | PAGE 100

The only time you should ever look back, is to see **HOW FAR** *you've come.*

THIS INSPIRES ME

Date: _____

TODAY I am grateful for

_____
_____
_____

My goal to keto success today is...

_____
_____
_____

One thing I appreciate about my keto journey today is

_____
_____
_____

Am I hydrated?								
	1	2	3	4	5	6	7	
	Good	Good	Fair	Dehydrated	Dehydrated	Very Dehydrated	Severe Dehydration	

RATE YOUR DAY

MOVE Today's workout	**NOURISH** Today's food	**REFLECT** Today's mood
Number of minutes	Energy Level 0 5 10	🙂 😐 🙁

GLUCOSE/KETONE Reading	**FASTING** Schedule	**SLEEP**

LOWCARBINSPIRATIONS.COM | PAGE 102

> **If you can dream it you can do it.**
> *Walt Disney*

THIS INSPIRES ME

Date: _____

TODAY I am grateful for

_____
_____

My goal to keto success today is...

_____
_____

One thing I appreciate about my keto journey today is

_____
_____

Am I hydrated?

1	2	3	4	5	6	7
Good	Good	Fair	Dehydrated	Dehydrated	Very Dehydrated	Severe Dehydration

RATE YOUR DAY

MOVE
Today's workout

Number of minutes _____

NOURISH
Today's food

Energy Level 0 — 5 — 10

REFLECT
Today's mood

:) :| :(

GLUCOSE/KETONE
Reading

FASTING
Schedule

SLEEP

LOWCARBINSPIRATIONS.COM | PAGE 104

THE BODY *achieves* WHAT THE MIND *believes*

THIS INSPIRES ME

My KETO MEAL PLAN

WEEK:

NOTES

B Breakfast L Lunch D Dinner

SUNDAY
- B
- L
- D

MONDAY
- B
- L
- D

TUESDAY
- B
- L
- D

WEDNESDAY
- B
- L
- D

THURSDAY
- B
- L
- D

FRIDAY
- B
- L
- D

SATURDAY
- B
- L
- D

My KETO MEAL PLAN

WEEK:

NOTES

B Breakfast · L Lunch · D Dinner

SUNDAY
- B
- L
- D

MONDAY
- B
- L
- D

TUESDAY
- B
- L
- D

WEDNESDAY
- B
- L
- D

THURSDAY
- B
- L
- D

FRIDAY
- B
- L
- D

SATURDAY
- B
- L
- D

My KETO MEAL PLAN

WEEK:

NOTES

B Breakfast **L** Lunch **D** Dinner

SUNDAY
- B
- L
- D

MONDAY
- B
- L
- D

TUESDAY
- B
- L
- D

WEDNESDAY
- B
- L
- D

THURSDAY
- B
- L
- D

FRIDAY
- B
- L
- D

SATURDAY
- B
- L
- D

My KETO MEAL PLAN

WEEK:

NOTES

B Breakfast L Lunch D Dinner

SUNDAY
- B
- L
- D

MONDAY
- B
- L
- D

TUESDAY
- B
- L
- D

WEDNESDAY
- B
- L
- D

THURSDAY
- B
- L
- D

FRIDAY
- B
- L
- D

SATURDAY
- B
- L
- D

NOTES

NOTES

NOTES

NOTES

NOTES

Made in the USA
Coppell, TX
05 January 2025